HOW TO PLAY OTAMATONE

CREATE ADDICTIVE, PLAYFUL MELODIES A STEP-BY-STEP GUIDE TO MASTERING IT.

copyright@2024

Quincy Sterling

Table of Contents

Introduction

Welcome to the fun magical world of Otamatone musical instrument; a completely unique one. The Otamatone is not just an instrument, but it feels like a journey that exceeds the limitations of conventional music. With a playful design and trademark sound, the Otamatone has taken the hearts of music lovers and thinking people alike. Visualize an instrument that looks like a strange combination of musical note and cheerful smile. This thin, stem-like structure decorated with a comical face holds the mystic elements that produce its unique yet fascinating sounds. Its uniqueness goes beyond appearance – the Otamatone is a highly-prized instrument that can imitate human voice, producing melodies ranging from silly to sinister.

In this ultimate guide, we set out on a quest to uncover the mysteries of Otamatone. If you are a novice and want to immerse yourself in the world of music or an experienced die-hard musician looking for new, unconventional muse this book is going to be your passport into learning how it's done with Otamatone .

In the pages that follow, you will learn to build and set up your Otamatone better than anyone else; in fact, not only all its secrets but also how a novice can play this extraordinary instrument on mastering some basic techniques of assembling it. The Otamatone is not only a musical instrument; it is an open call to be creative, make up your own melodies and become attached with the charm of setting this quirky creature in motion through contacting its various parts.

Get ready to be enthralled, enchanted and inspired as we take you into the fascinating world of Otamatone. Let the journey begin!

Purpose of the Book:

This book is a specialized guide created to arm individuals with the knowledge and skills required in becoming Otamatone masters. In the world full of musical opportunities, Otamatone is a rather peculiar and interesting instrument; this guide would be your ally on the path to being an expert at mastering how it works.

Our purpose is clear: to offer a one-stop solution that turns dreaming musicians into pro Otamatone players with the power of written words alone. As opposed to normal music guides that depend on sound samples, this book adopts a literary perspective using descriptive language , notations and diagrams in an attempt to relate the intricacies of playing the Otamatone.

By taking a walk through an organized sequence of well-structured chapters, you will be able to take your exploration process one step at a time about the hows and why there are certain things that come together to form the instrument, methods or ways in which it is played, evening notes among other musical aspects. Each section is thoroughly structured to provide useful knowledge, turning you into an expert Otamatone beginner.

The appeal of this method lies in its simplicity. It offers opportunities for both beginners wanting to start their musical career and musicians who are already familiar with this field but looking forward to a new exciting challenge. the technicalities involved in playing an Otamatone but you will also be confident and inspirited to compose your own tunes by the time you reach last pages.

In short, this book opens a door through which people can enter to discover the expressive power latent in an Otamatone and build a community of players who are charmed by its playful magic and unmatched musical capacities. Get ready to plunge into the written realm of the Otamatone and let words be your guide on a fulfilling and profitable musical journey.

Chapter 1

Getting Started

Welcome to first chapter of your learning path towards mastering the world of Otamatone. So, before we go on the specifics of playing this weird instrument itself, let's lay a good solid foundation by knowing what its parts are and how to set it up in order for them all to play together delightfully.

1.1 Overview of the Otamatone:

The Otamatone is an amusing combination of creativity and music. With its design resembling a musical note and having a smiling face, it is an obvious sign of the joy that comes with using it. After first glance, you'll see main components that make its peculiar look and sound.

1.1.1 Stem:

The Otamatone' elongated stem acts as both its body and grip. It is in this section that magic takes place it houses the hardware components of the instrument necessary for creating sound.

1.1.2 Notehead:

The notehead marks the summit of the stem, lending a little personality to Otamatone design. Here, you will locate the pitch control mechanism that enables you to play around with the tone and pitch of this musical instrument.

1.1.3 Mouth:

The Otamatone has a smiling face just below the notehead. This mouth is much more than just a fanciful gimmick – it houses the sound hole, and serves an absolutely critical function in producing those vocal-like characteristics for which Otamatone instruments are renowned.

1.2 Assembling Your Otamatone:

Now you are familiar with the parts of Otamatone, let us move on to assembling it. Follow these simple steps to set up your Otamatone for an enjoyable playing experience

1.2.1 Attaching the Notehead:

Screw the notehead lightly on top of the stem while making sure it fits snugly. This step is crucial for the accurate control of pitch when playing.

1.2.2 Checking the Batteries:

Make sure to confirm that the batteries are properly installed in your Otamatone and they work if it has electronic features. This makes the sound output to be consistent and clear.

1.2.3 Adjusting the Mouth:

Try the different positions of mouth to understand how this will sound in difference tonalities. These subtle modifications can entirely change the sound's quality.

1.3 Understanding the Controls:

Before setting out on our quest for music, it is wise to get acquainted with the controls that will define our sonic discovery.

1.3.1 Pitch Control:

The pitch control slider is positioned on the notehead and allows you to modify the Otamatone's tune. Move it upwards or downwards to browse the wide spectrum of tones, generating your choice of melodies.

1.3.2 Volume Control:

A lot of Otamatones have a volume control knob — it's usually located near the base of the stem. Play around with this knob to discover the right level for your playing surroundings.

1.3.3 Power Switch:

If your Otamatone has electronic components, find the power switch and make sure it is set to "on". This turns on all the integrated features and lets you enjoy your instrument to its fullest.

1.4 Otamatone in Action:

Having assembled your Otamatone and learned about how to use it, let's take a short journey on the instrument in action.

1.4.1 Basic Sound Production:

Press the touch-sensitive strip gently on top of the notehead to produce your first sounds. Play with various levels of pressure to find the subtleties regarding volume and emotion.

1.4.2 Exploring Pitch:

Alter the pitch of sound produced by sliding the pitch control. Explore the whole range, from high-pitched whimsy to low, resonant tones – take your time with it.

1.4.3 Getting Comfortable:

Pick up your Otamatone such a way that you are comfortable and there is easy access to the controls. This comfort is necessary for easy and pleasant game sessions.

1.5 Next Steps:

Coming to the end of this chapter you not only have built your Otamatone but also learned a basic knowledge about its parts and functions. In the subsequent chapters, we'll explore basic playing techniques that will arm you with knowledge and skills to enable expression on this remarkable instrument.

It's time to release the full potential of your Otamatone as we guide you through each phase of your musical endeavors. Whether you're new to music or a seasoned musician, the Otamatone guarantees singular and enjoyable journey. So, stay tuned for the following chapter because here we discuss basic techniques that will lay groundwork of your future mastering of Otamatone.

Putting and Assembling Your Otamatone

Here is the practical side of your Otamatone experience! In this part, we will take you through the process of building and mounting your Otamatone to make music a joyable thing.

Unboxing Your Otamatone:

When you first get your Otamatone, it generally arrives disassembled so that it can be safely shipped. Open the packaging carefully, and you'll find the main components: So, the stem, notehead and any other accessories.

Attaching the Notehead:

The pitch control mechanism lies in the notehead of your Otamatone. To assemble:

1. Take the notehead and locate the screw thread at the bottom.

2. Ensure that the screw thread matches with the hole at stem's top.

3. Screw lightly the notehead onto the stem in a clockwise manner until it is tight.

Provide a snug fit, but do not tighten too much otherwise you will damage the threads.

Powering Up (if applicable):

If you have an electronic Otamatone, it may need batteries. Check out the manufacturer's instructions regarding that particular type of battery and how to mount it. Typically, the battery compartment can be found on the stem or in some notehead.

1. Open the battery compartment and place batteries in it with regard to polarity indicators.

2. Close the compartment securely.

If your Otamatone does not have electronic features, this step can be omitted.

Checking the Mouth Position:

The mouth on the Otamatone is both a fantastic design aspect as well and serves as the sound hole. Experiment with its position to influence the sound characteristics:

1. Move slightly up or lower the mouth, but gently.

2. Play and listen to how the sounds change.

In this small change you can greatly affect the tonal sounds your Otamatone will produce.

Ready to Play:

When your notehead is attached, batteries inserted if necessary and the mouth mounted; you are ready to play with your Otamatone.

1. Place the Otamatone comfortably on your laps to reach controls easily enough.

2. Familiarize yourself with the pitch and volume knobs.

3. Gently rub the touch-sensitive strip on the notehead to get your first notes.

Maintenance Tips:

Before we get into playing techniques, let's briefly discuss a few basic maintenance tips that should be done to maintain your Otamatone in perfect shape.

1. Cleaning:

Frequently clean the Otamatone surface using a soft, dry cloth to remove dust and debris. For stubborn stains, a cloth that is slightly damp can be used but do not let electronic components get in contact with moisture.

2. Storage:

Store your Otamatone in a cool and dry place when not using it. If possible, store it in its original packaging or a protective case to avoid any scratches and dust accumulations.

3. Battery Care:

If your Otamatone uses batteries, make sure to take them out when you're not using it for a long time. This prevents some battery leakage that might ruin the electronic parts.

4. Notehead Alignment:

Regularly check alignment of the notehead to make sure it is safely connected. If you see any loose fitting, just pull it slightly to make sure its still connected firmly.

Troubleshooting:

You may still find some minor problems despite proper care. Here are some common troubleshooting tips:

1. Inconsistent Sound:

If your Otamatone has electronic features, check the batteries. Inconsistent sound may appear due to low battery power. Make sure the touch-sensitive strip on a non electric Otamatone is clean.

2. Pitch Control Issues:

If the pitch control slider feels stiff or unresponsive, lubricate lightly with type of lube recommended by manufacturer. Do not use your strength because it can damage the mechanism.

3. Unusual Sounds:

Investigate any strange sounds by looking into the internal parts. Loose parts may produce rattling noises. screws or ask for help from professionals.

Conclusion:

With your Otamatone assembled, set up and with a basic understanding of maintenance tips you can now start the fun journey of mastering this quirky instrument.

Brace yourself for an interactive journey as we walk you through the twists and turns of Otamatone playing. The adventure just started, and your Otamatone is ready to feel your musical touch!

Basic Music Terminology:

So that we turn ourselves to the details of playing Otamatone, let's learn some basic music terms. These terms will be a useful starting point for anyone who is new to the music world to understand what all these instructions and concepts presented in the forthcoming chapters mean.

Pitch:

- Definition: The perceived pitch of a sound involving the frequency that determines if it's high or low.

- Example: By touching the touch-sensitive strip on the Otamatone's notehead, you can alter its emitted sound as for pitch.

Note:

- Definition: This is a symbol that represents pitch and duration of notes in the music notation.

- Example: Sheet music contains notes, which are expressed as circles with stems and flags. The pitch is higher with a note placed on the staff further up.

Rhythm:

- Definition: Rhythm is the organization of sounds and silences in music based on length.

- Example: You can clap your hands to a steady beat, which implies rhythms of some sort.

Dynamics:

- Definition: The wide range of loudness and silence in music.

- Example: By playing the Otamatone with a greater force on contact surface results in volume change.

Tempo:

- Definition: The tempo at which a music piece is played.

- Example: Allegro is fast tempo and Adagio slow tempo.

Melody:

- Definition: A row of individual pitches that constitute a musical phrase.

- Example: "Twinkle, Twinkle little star" is a simple tune used to teach beginners.

Harmony:

- Definition: or sung at the same time.

- Example: Several Otamatones can be played simultaneously to produce harmonious sounds.

Staff:

- Definition: A stave of horizontal lines and spaces on which musical notes are inscribed.
- Example: Sheet music uses a staff to notate the pitch of notes in which higher pitches are placed on top.

Clef:

- Definition: A mark on the staff to denote a pitch range.
- Example: Higher-pitched instruments including the Otamatone are often notated using treble clef.

Otamatone-Specific Terminology:

Apart from regular music vocabulary, you should also acquaint yourself with some of the Otamatone-specific terms that will appear rather often in this guide.

Touch-Sensitive Strip:

- Definition: The touch-sensitive part of the notehead that produces sound when pressed on the Otamatone.
- Usage: Use a gentle press on the touch-sensitive strip to initiate sound production.

Pitch Control:

- Definition: the mechanism, often a slider which alters its pitch; The Otamatone.

- Usage: Try adjusting the pitch control slider to uncover various tones.

Notehead:

- Definition:The upper part of the Otamatone that holds pitch control mechanism and gives it its unique look.

- Usage: Make sure the notehead is well affixed to the stem so as to serve its purpose.

Vibrato:

- Definition: Regular, pulsating alteration of pitch.

 - Usage: Try adding vibrato by lightly sliding your finger along the pressure-sensitive strip as you play.

Dynamics on the Otamatone:

- Definition: Pressures on the touch-sensitive strip produced volume variations.

- Usage: Play a variety of dynamics on the Otamatone by pressing in areas with different degree of pressure.

Recap:

Having a basic knowledge of both general music terms and the unique terminology associated with Otamatone, you are now ready to explore your playing technique for this special musical instrument. These terms will act as your musical vocabulary while we go through the various techniques and concepts in our next chapters.

Chapter 2
Playing Techniques

Join us on your Otamatone adventure as we explore the playing techniques that will take you to the heart of this charming instrument. In this chapter, we'll uncover a variety of methods that bring its whimsical character to life. From mastering button presses to refining pitch control, each technique plays an integral role in shaping the unique sonic spectrum of the Otamatone.

2.1 Mastering Button Presses:

At center stage is our touch-sensitive notehead strip which responds seamlessly and swiftly according to pressure applied by your fingers. Divided into segments with distinct pitches assigned systematically throughout; it's imperative for any budding musician aspiring towards melody-playing mastery -to have fluency at navigating these core features!

1. Pressing a Single Segment:

- Technique: Apply gentle pressure to one segment on the touch-sensitive strip.

- Effect: One note is produced at the pitch that corresponds with the selected segment.

2. Sequential Segment Presses:

- Technique: Tap multiple segments in order, touching each consecutively.

- Effect: A melody of individual notes are played within a sequence; creating musical harmony through an ordered pattern.

3. Chord Input via Simultaneous Segments' Pressure

- Methodology Needed for Execution:"Press simultaneously several adjacent or non-contiguous elements"

Inclusion Of Information Regarding Actual Instrument Being Referred To May Be Necessary Depending On The Context

4.Glissando Motion Utilizing Touch-Sensitive Strip's SurfaceArea

Method and/or Steps Involved:

"Slide your finger smoothly across responsive surface areas horizontally (or over other spatial planes) while maintaining constant contact."

Resultant Musical Output/Effect :

Pitch alteration ranging from low-to-high(and vice versa), almost continuously producing as if it were conveying sound effects characterized by sliding motion

The Otamatone's notehead houses a pitch control slider that can produce a wide variety of tones, making it crucial to master for conveying different emotions through your music. Here are some techniques and effects you can achieve:

1. Upward Slide: Sliding the pitch control upwards results in higher, brighter notes.

2. Downward Slide: Pulling the slide down produces deeper and mellower sounds.

3. Vibrato with Pitch Control: Oscillating your finger while maintaining contact with the strip introduces subtle vibrato by modulating pitches.

To take full advantage of this instrument's capabilities, incorporate multiple techniques together like so:

1. Chord Progressions: By sequentially pressing buttons on the Otamatone, chord progressions become effortless- spicing up melodies to make them interesting.

2.Dynamic Slides; One can combine changes in button pressure coupled wiothpitch slides tone fluctuations resultingin expressive musical phrases

2.4 Example Exercises to Practice:

1. Improvisation:

- Begin with a basic melody consisting of just one note and experiment by adding sequential notes.

2. Chord Progression Training:

- Combine multiple segments simultaneously to create harmonious chords, then work on transitioning between different chord shapes.

3. Pitch Modulation Exercise:

 - While holding down a sustained note, practice sliding the pitch control slider up and down in order to develop better control over pitch modulation.

4.Duplicating Songs:

- Choose an easily recognizable song and replicate it via use of button presses along with alterations using pitch controls.

2.5 Conclusion:

By completing these exercises included within this chapter you should be well equipped for embarking upon your Otamatone playing journey! Improving through mastery of such skills is what will enable self-expression as well guide you towards exploring all musical possibilities offered through utilization thereof – setting out towards applying specific techniques from future chapters into diverse genres or even ultimately creating original music compositions. With playful experimentation the transformation possible shall indeed delightfully breathe life into any piece played. Immerse yourself-- One delightful tune at-a-time !

Practicing Playing Techniques: Exercises to Refine Your Skills

After learning about the different playing techniques for your Otamatone, it's time to put them into practice with exercises that will help improve your skills. These practical drills focus on button presses, pitch control and how they can be used together.

2.6 Button Pressing Drills:

Exercise 1 - Single Note Warm-up

Select a segment on the touch-sensitive strip. Repeatedly press and release different segments while exploring various pitches available.

Exercise 2 - Sequential Press Challenge

Choose an easy melody or use a scale as if you were performing.

Play each note by pressing buttons sequentially without missing one but ensuring smooth transitions between notes despite complexity increase over periods of practice sessions.

Exercise 3 – Chord Mastery Exploration & Practice

Experiment using multiple simultaneous key combinations resulting in chords creation from this experimentation gradually develop mastery levels moving along common chord progressions (major/minor/seventh), perfect these new-found abilities trying switch sheets seamlessly altogether during playtime exercise.

2.7 Pitch Control Maneuvers Exercise:
 Exercise four tests players' ability; Hold out sustained notes sliding upward/downward degrees via manipulation of the slider until comfy experimenting speed length shifts pair up well with sequenced markings provide unique interpretation audio expressions wherever desired.

Step five takes things even further combining sequential loopings with subtle/predominant vibrato variations incomparably supplemented alongside above-explained maneuvers/methods saw earlier tries twofold fast changes here when integrated variables are subjected alike its impact becomes more grandiose duo-fervour elements suitable pairs helping necessary highlighting difference expressive phrasing imponderable results paired harmoniously..

Example Of Complete Session:

Start off warming up single-notes sequences Drill One specifically implemented empirical test knowledge presently relaxed; thereby assisting first attempts placement at adequate curates enough material(recording)?... Continue progressing towards increasingly difficult melodies continually integrate progressive approach simplified methodology masterfully maintaining core principles.

Afterwards, including chord shapes/sequences Drill Three prompting to try incorporation additional elements focusing upon pitch joining smooth transitions thereof via the indulgement of creative ingenuity available allowing expressive phrasing modulation using various techniques wider expressions bloom into play...

2.10 Concluding Thoughts:

Indeed you've come quite far but remember laying this solid foundation whilst consistently practicing it thoroughly will only aid improve your technical proficiency and also open more possibilities in pursuit becoming a professional Otamatone musician.. Further advanced diversified genre embrace vigorously infused personal style/substance climb highest levels surpass anything ever thought possible genuine musical journey inspiration motivation achieved nothing short pure joy tried emulating until now...

Chapter 3

Understanding Otamatone Notation

Let's discover the enchanting universe of
Otamatone notation. In this section, we'll delve
into an uncomplicated system that enables you to
interpret and play music explicitly tailored for your
Otamatone device effortlessly. With our custom-
made notation as your guide, navigating through
melodies, harmonies and dynamics will be a
breeze.

3.1 The Otamatone Stave:

Our simplified version involves using one single
stave line rather than multiple ones so interpreting
notes on the staff is straightforward when playing
with an Otamotane instrument: Each point along
the horizontal axis corresponds neatly to specific
sections across your touch-sensitive strip placed
upon its notehead- whereby higher points denote
greater pitches high in soundscape dimensions.

3.2 Pitch Markings:

Fittingly representing individual tones become effortless thanks to numbers 1through 8 utilized within our pitch marking scheme which aligns seamlessly alongside each segment drawn out from your trusty devices' touchscreen.The corresponding numerical values are assigned according

to these precise eight sound varieties:

Un   - No Sound(No Touch).

Ni   - Half Step above

Nopitch(lowest)

Do   - First Note From Bottom

(Low)

Re   – Second Note

Mi   – ThirdNote

Fa   – Fourth(Note Just Above

Mi)

Sol   --Fifth Notes

La   --Sixthnote

Ti   --Seventh

Ho   Highest octave audible by
human ears(Eighth).

- 1: Lowest pitch

- 2:

- 3:

- 4:

- 5:

- 6:

- 7:

- 8: Highest pitch

3.3 Single Notes:

For single notes, a number on the staff indicates
the segment you should press. The duration of the
note is represented by its visual length on the staff:
Example 1: Playing Segment 4 for a quarter note

|| **4**

||

||

3.4 Chords:

Chords are shown through vertical stacking of numbers. Each number refers to the press segment that should be pressed simultaneously. The vertical alignment signifies that these segments should be played together:

Example 2: Playing Chord 3 and 5 together

|| 3

|| 5

||

3.5 Pitch Control:

The corresponding pitch control will be indicated by an arrow pointing upward (↑) or downward ↓ This guides you to slide the pitch control slider in the indicated direction:

Example 3: Playing the Segment 6 , use slide pitch control upward.

|| 6 ↑

||

||

3.6 Dynamics:

Dynamics, or changes in volume, are indicated by placing a small "f" for forte (loud) or "p" for piano (soft) next to the number:

Example 4: Play Segment 2 loudly

|| 2 f

||

||

3.7 Example Musical Phrases:

Now, let's apply our notation to a short musical phrase:

Example 5: Musical Phrase

|| 3

|| 5

|| 3 f

|| 6 ↑

|| 4

|| 2 p

||

In this instance, we play a chord – Segments 3 and 5 sounds together; after that, one note is noticed loud (forte) or sounded Segment -please pass the</s> closes by playing loudly … withdraw to drop out i.

3.8 Conclusion:

Now you have a simplified Otamatone notation system that acts as the visual means of interpreting and playing music unique to this quirky instrument. Practice reading straightforward melodies and chords with this notation, and soon you will be able to convert written music into beautiful Otamatone sounds. Along the way, you will learn about more complex notation ideas and even compose your own pieces of music. As you embark further on your Otamatone journey into the land of tunes and chords, let this notation show you the way!

3.9 Rhythmic Notation:

Now, let's explore how we can introduce rhythm into our notation system. We will indicate note values on our one-line musical staff with simple rhythmic symbols.

- Whole Note: Represented by a circle.

- Half Note: It is represented by a circle with a stem.

- Quarter Note: Filled circle with a stem.

- Eighth Note: It is represented by a full circle with stem + flag.

3.10 Combining Pitch and Rhythm:

Let's extend our notation to include rhythm in our musical phrases:

Example 6: Musical Phrase with Rhythm

|| 3 4 2

|| 5 6 4

|| 3 f 4 2

|| 6 ↑ 4 2 p

|| 4

|| 2

||

In this particular case, we have introduced rhythm into the notation. Despite this, the figures still denote sections to be played; whereas rhythmic symbols specify how long each note should last.

3.11 Tie and Dot Notation:

We add tie and dot notation to increase rhythmic intricacy.

- Tie: A line that meanders between two notes of identical pitch, representing the playing of those notes as a combined note or a long tone.

- Dot: Used after the note to prolong it by half.

Example 7: Tie and Dot Notation

|| 3 4 2

|| 5 6 4

|| 3 f 4 2

|| 6 ↑ 4 2 p

|| 4

|| 2.

||

In this example, a tie connects two Segment 2 notes, creating a sustained sound. The dot after the Segment 2 note extends its duration.

3.12 Rests:

Silences, or rests, are essential in music notation. We'll use symbols to represent rests on our single-line staff.

- Whole Rest: A rectangle positioned below the line.

- Half Rest: A rectangle positioned above the line.

- Quarter Rest: A diagonal line through the line.

Example 8: Introducing Rests

|| 3 4 2

|| 5 6 4

|| 3 f 4 2

|| 6 ↑ 4 2 p

|| 4

|| 2.

|| 4

||

In this example, we've added quarter rests to represent silent beats between the notes.

3.13 Conclusion:

Now that we have included rhythm, ties, dots and rests our Otamatone notation system becomes complete. Then practice reading and playing out musical phrases in different rhythms, and soon enough you will be able to interpret many kinds of written music for the Otamatone. In the following chapters, we'll delve deeper into more sophisticated notation techniques and help you perform complex pieces of music. So relax and take the rhythmical journey into playful world of Otamatones music.

Understanding Otamatone Notation - Reading and Interpretation

Now that we have created a simplified system of Otamatone notation, let's delve into the intricacies and art of reading music written specifically for this quirky musical instrument. Knowing how to move through the musical phrases, identifying various symbols and understanding expressive aspects of music is crucial in giving life to written compositions with your Otamatone.

3.14 Reading Music:
Reading music for the Otamatone is a combination of pitch, rhythm and some more symbols. 1st step, 2nd step etc.

1. Identify Pitches:

- The numbers in the single-line staff are the segments on your notehead of Otamatone.

- Identify the pitch range by linking higher staff mark with high pitches and vice versa.

2. Decipher Rhythmic Patterns:

- Identify the rhythmic symbols for whole, half quarter and eighth notes.

- Understand how the numbers interact with these symbols to decide both pitch and duration.

3. Explore Ties and Dots:

- Find links between two equivalent notes, showing a prolonged sound.

- Notice dots after notes, which give them the duration of half.

4. Account for Rests:

- Identify rest symbols for whole , half, and quarter rests to indicate silent beats used between notes.

3.15 Interpretation:

Music interpretation is not as simple as reading the notes. It involves putting some more character and personality into your delivery. Here are key elements to consider:

1. Dynamics:

- Be aware of dynamics symbols (f – forte, p – piano) to differentiate the volume you will play.

- Experiment with the contrast of different pressure levels on the touch-sensitive strip.

2. Pitch Control Instructions:

- "Press jump (↑ for upward slides, ↓ for downward ones) to perform pitch control moves.

- combine the control of pitch with button presses for a subtle and emotional performance.

3. Vibrato and Articulation:

- Apply vibrato in sections where you think it will add a slight touch of expressiveness.

- Consider rubato, articulation markings such as staccato dots and legato lines to shape the overall phrasing of your performance.

3.16 Example Interpretation:

Let's revisit a previous musical phrase example and interpret it:

Example 9: Interpretation of a Musical Phrase

|| 3 4 2

|| 5 6 4

|| 3 f 4 2

|| 6 ↑ 4 2 p

|| 4

|| 2.

||

Interpretation:

- Start with a medium level (f) of Segment 3 .

- 3 and 5 segments – Transition to a louder (f) chord.

- ↑ Segment 6 slide.

- Play Segment 4 pianissimo (p) with a legato touch downwards.

- Play Segment 2 mezzo-piano (p) with a dotted half note.

3.17 Practice Tips:
1. Start Slow:

- Start with simple phrases in a slow tempo.

- Focus on getting notation into sound.

2. Gradually Increase Complexity:

- As your reading skills improve progress to more complicated pieces.

- Set different rhythms and markings for dynamics.

3. Experiment with Expression:

- Address the communicative aspects in the notation.

- Add character by experimenting with vibrato, dynamic changes and pitch control.

3.18 Conclusion:

As you begin reading and deciphering Otamatone songs, be aware that it's not enough to simply copy the notes put down on paper—it is more important to bring your own individual spin or character into each performance. While the notation may guide you, your creativity and expression become what draws the heart of music. In the following chapters we will discuss particular styles, enhanced methods and show you how to produce your music with Otamatone. Bring your written notes to life and bring them fun with playful, whimsy sounds of Otamatone.

Chapter 4

Basic Songs and Melodies

In this chapter, we will explore some easy songs and tunes that can be used by beginners to practice and improve their Otamatone abilities. Other songs which are chosen very carefully embrace button presses, pitch control and rhythmic factor. Let's go through each part by the piece to make sure you haven't left any stone unturned in your musical adventure with Otamatone.

4.1 Song 1: "Twinkle, Twinkle, Little Star"

Melody:

|| 1 1 5 5
|| 6 6 5
|| 4 4 3 3
|| 2 2 1
||

Practice Tips:

1. Start by playing each note gradually to become accustomed to the tune.

2. Once you are at ease, gradually pick up the tempo.

3. Use the touch-sensitive strip to experiment with dynamic changes.

4. Add a light pitch control glide at the end of phrases for an added playfulness.

4.2 Song 2: "Happy Birthday"

Melody:

|| 3 3 4 3 6 5

|| 3 3 4 3 7 6

|| 3 3 8 6 4 4

|| 3 3 4 3 6 5

||

Practice Tips:

1. more attention should be given to the rhythmic structure of that melody.

2. Play the melody at a moderate tempo before increasing speed.

3. Use pitch control slides on the sustained notes and experiment.

4. Add dynamics, to put emphasis on such phrases as the first and last lines.

4.3 Song 3: "Mary Had a Little Lamb"

Melody:

|| 3 2 1 2 3 3 3

|| 2 2 2 3 5 5

|| 3 3 3 2 2 2

|| 3 2 1 2 3 3 3

||

Practice Tips:

1. Observe the recurring rhythmic pattern.

2. Play with a steady tempo and gradually get faster.

3. Use dynamics to make the performance playful and dynamic.

4. Add vibrato to long notes for emphasis.

4.4 Song 4: "Jingle Bells"

Melody:

|| 3 3 3 3 3 3 3 5 1 2 2 2 2 2 2

|| 1 1 1 1 1 1 3 1 5 5 5 4 4 3 3

|| 3 3 3 3 3 3 3 5 1 2 2 2 2 2 2

|| 1 1 1 1 1 3 1 5 5 5 4 4 3 3 3
||

Practice Tips:

1. Break down the melody into segments that can be learned more easily.

2. Try pitch control slides or dynamic variations.

3. Characterize the chorus section by rhythmic pattern.

4. Play slowly, then gradually increase speed.

4.5 Song 5: "Let It Go" (From Frozen)

Melody:

|| 5 5 6 8 8 6 5 3 3 5 5 6 8 8 6
5 3

|| 5 5 6 8 8 6 5 3 3 5 5 6 8 8 6
5 3

|| 3 3 4 6 6 4 3 2 2 3 3 4 6 6 4
3 2

|| 1 1 2 3 3 2 1 7 7 1 1 2 3 3 2
1 7

||

Practice Tips:

1. Break down the melody into sections for focused practice.

2. Focus on the dynamics changes in every phrase.

3. Apply vibrato on sustained notes to produce a more inspiring performance.

4. 4 Add empathetic pitch slides to make it smooth and emotional.

4.6 Conclusion:
These elementary songs and tunes offer a rich palette of practice resources for children learning to play Otamatone. Handle each piece with patience, working on mastering one before moving to the other. Try to experiment with dynamics, control the pitch and incorporate your personal elements of expressiveness into each performance.

As you learn, do not mind the alterations and how to create your arrangments using these songs in a way that best fits with what suits The following pages will explore more sophisticated techniques, genres and help you develop yours

Basic Songs and Melodies - Step-by-Step Instructions

Let's give detailed instructions on how to play each of the basic songs and melodies covered in this chapter. With these instructions, you can make your way through the Otamatone one note at a time.

4.1 Song 1: "Twinkle, Twinkle, Little Star"

Step-by-Step Instructions:

1. Start with Segment 1. Gently press it to create the first tone.

2. 2nd Note Go to Segment 6.

3. Third note following Segment 5.

4. Continue with the pattern, playing each note in sequence.

5. Experiment with dynamic changes of sound, try playing some notes louder (forte) and others softer.

6. To add a playful tone, introduce a discreet pitch control slide at the conclusion of the phrase.

4.2 Song 2: "Happy Birthday"

Step-by-Step Instructions:

1. Start with Segment 3, and play it for the first two beats.

2. On the next two beats, move to Segment 4.

3. To form the first line, go through Segment 3, followed by 6 and eventually finish with number .

4. Follow this segment for the following lines, as indicated.

5. Try pitch control slides on sustained notes to add a dynamic touch.

6. Spice up the emphasis by playing some notes louder (forte) and softer(piano).

4.3 Song 3: "Mary Had a Little Lamb"

Step-by-Step Instructions:

1. 3, 2, 1 and then ends with number "2" in the first line.

2. Move to line 3,5,3,2 and 14.

3. Use this pattern for the following lines.

4. Keep a steady beat, slowly getting faster as you get better.

5. Play with dynamics, adding an expressive flourish to the legato passages.

6. Introduce vibrato on long notes for that extra expressive touch.

4.4 Song 4: "Jingle Bells"

Step-by-Step Instructions:

1. 3 Segment, play one time.

2. 3-beat transition to Segment 5.

3. For the next series of notes move to Segment 1, then 2.

4. Following the specified segments, repeat this pattern for other lines.

5. Pay attention to the rhythmic structure in chorus section, but keep steady beat.

6. Make the performance lively by attempting pitch control slides and dynamic variations.

4.5 Song 5: "Let It Go" (From Frozen)

Step-by-Step Instructions:

1. 5, 6 ,Then 8 & then again the number six for this first phrase.

2. For the next phrase, move to Segment 5,6.

3. Repeat this pattern for subsequent lines, following the indicated segments.

4. Focus on the rhythmic changes of every phrase, playing loudly (forte) or gently (piano), as specified.

5. Sustain notes and add vibrato for a more expressive sound.

6. Use pitch control slides in order to create flowing and emotional phrases.

4.6 Conclusion:

For each song, work on precision and expression step by step. Start with a comfortable pace, and as you gain confidence increase the speed. These songs are intended to be the solid base for your Otamatone capabilities, introducing different techniques and musical elements.

Feel free to re-evaluate every piece, try out various interpretations and personalize the performances.

As you proceed, the forthcoming chapters will bring advanced techniques, genres and assist in crafting your compositions. Have fun in the process of learning to play these simple songs and melodias on your Otamatone!

Chapter 5

Advanced Techniques

In this chapter we will explore more advanced techniques that will take your Otamatone playing to the next level of expressiveness and sophistication. These techniques are beyond basic, they add subtlety to your performance allowing you the freedom of injecting yourself into everyone note.

5.1 Vibrato:

Definition: Vibrato is when you wobble the pitch of a sustained note to make a very slight pulsed sound.

How to Execute:

1. Play a long sustained note on the Otamatone.

2. Touch the touch-sensitive strip gently and "swing" finger about it slowly with contact.

Example:

```
||  5 ~
||
||
```

```
```
Practice Tips:

- Start with slow and steady vibrato.

- Try fast and slow neck vibration with high or low intensity.

- Use vibrato sparingly, but use it to create a distinctive character in sustained notes.

5.2 Dynamics Variation:

Definition: Varying the dynamics means that you can play louder or softer to provide a sense of emotion in your music.

How to Execute:

1. A touch-sensitive strip is used to adjust the pressure and control volume.

2. Press harder for fortissimo and lighter fir piano.

Example:

```
|| 3 f
 ||
--||
```
```
```
Practice Tips:

- Try playing segments of a phrase at different volumes.

- Make certain notes or phrases bold with dynamics.

- Practice soft-hard transitions.

5.3 Pitch Bending:

Definition: Pitch bending refers to the process of altering a note's pitch smoothly and gradually, resulting in some kind bent or slid effect.

How to Execute:

1. Choose a note on the Otamatone.

2. Gradually touch the strip with your finger to adjust its pitch.

Example:

```
||  6 ↕
||
--||
```
```

Practice Tips:

- –Experiment with different durations and ranges of pitch bending.
```

- Try adding pitch bends to melodic phrases.

- Connect two completely different notes smoothly via pitch bending.

5.4 Staccato and Legato:

Definitions:

- Staccato refers to playing a note which is short and detached.

- Legato refers to the playing of notes smoothly without spaces between them.

How to Execute:

1. Staccato: Press a segment and lift your finger rapidly.

2. Legato: Minimise the gap between notes and connect them smoothly.

Example:

|| **4 . 5 . 6**

||

Practice Tips:

- Try using staccato and legato within a phrase.

- Make it staccato to convey a playful and percussive effect.

- Use legato for a smooth sounding of notes while they connect.

5.5 Example Incorporating Advanced Techniques:

Example:

```
|| 3 f 4 ~ 6 ↑ 4 . 5 . 6 ↕
  ||
--||
```
```

**Interpretation:**

1. Segment 3 is moderately loud (forte).

2. Use vibrato on the held note in Segment 4.

3. 6 Perform an upward pitch control slide.

4. 4, 5 and 6 are segments play a staccato pattern.

5. Start to bend the pitch downwards on Segment 6.

**5.6 Conclusion:**
These techniques make your Otamatone playing more expressive. As you develop vibrato, dynamics change, pitch bending staccato and leg ,
```

bear in mind to add your personal flair into every rendition. Practice these techniques in isolation and then bring them together to establish vibrant musical creations.

In the chapters that successively follow, we are going to use these advanced techniques on certain genres and guide you in creating richer and more sophisticated Otamatone compositions. Use these advanced techniques to enjoy the journey of unleashing in full your Otamatone's potential.

Advanced Techniques - Exercises and Examples

In order to master the advanced techniques that will be introduced in this chapter, it is essential to focus on specific exercises and study practical cases. With these exercises, you will have the skill and confidence to play with vibrato dynamics variation pitch bending staccato and legato on your Otamatone.

5.7 Vibrato Exercise:

Exercise: Vibrato Control

1. Play a long note on the Otamatone.

2. Play a controlled vibrato by moving your finger on the touch-sensitive strip.

3. Begin with a slow and wide sweep, gain speed over time and vary the vibrato width.

4. To improve your vibrato control, repeat the exercise with varying notes.

5.8 Dynamics Variation Exercise:

Exercise: Dynamic Phrasing

1. Choose a short melody or phrase.

2. Play each note softly piano and loud forte.

3. Experiment with some sudden dynamic shifts and others more gradual transitions.

4. Concentrate on keeping a steady and smooth touch across the touch-sensitive strip when changing pressure.

5.9 Pitch Bending Exercise:

Exercise: Pitch Bend Exploration

1. Choose a sustained note.

2. Practice pitch bending by moving your finger up and down on the touch-sensitive strip.

3. Experiment with different pitch bend durations and ranges.

4. Explore the expressive potential of short melodic phrases that incorporate pitch bending.

5.10 Staccato and Legato Exercise:

Exercise: Staccato-Legato Fusion

1. By a melody of short and long notes.

2. For each note, alternate between staccato and legato articulations.

3. Focus on lifting your finger quickly for staccato and connecting notes smoothly for legato.

4. With time, increase the complexity of sequence.

5.11 Example Incorporating Exercises:

Example:

|| 3 f 4 ~ 6 ↑ 4 . 5 . 6 ↕

||

--||

```
```

Interpretation with Exercises:

1. Start controlled vibrato on the moderately loud (forte) Segment 3.

2. ↑ Perform a slow pitch bend on Segment 6.

3. Short, detached pattern with Segments 4,5 and so forth can be played staccato.

4. Incorporate dynamics variation by playing the Segment 4 pianissimo after staccato.

5. Connect the sustained note on Segment 6 with a legato connection to Segment .

6. Conclude with a pitch bend downward (↕) on Segment 6.

5.12 Conclusion:

Taking part in these drill and investigating the example will help you master advanced techniques on Otamatone . As with all techniques, consistent practice is crucial to refining the finesse required for seamlessly executing these in the many musical contexts.

As you move along, try creating your own exercises using these techniques applied to the tunes or compositions which are dear for you. In the next chapters, we will use these techniques on specific types of music allowing you to perform Otamatone in a diversified and emotional manner. Savor the exploration and development of high level techniques on your Otamatone path!

Chapter 6

Creating Your Own Music

In this chapter, we'll start a creative ride as I shall guide you through the process of creating your own Otamatone music. For a beginner or an experienced player, nothing is more democratic and rewarding than to bring your own musical ideas into fruition by composition. Firstly, let's consider the steps you might take to bring your musical dream into reality on the eccentric platform of Otamatone.

6.1 Inspiration and Concept:
Explore Ideas:

1. Begin by brainstorming musical ideas. Take into account the mood, theme or emotion you want to portray.

2. Use your experiences, emotions or other music pieces that touch you as inspiration.

3. Consider the playful nature of the Otamatone and how you will incorporate that into your composition.

Create a Concept:

1. Develop a concept for your composition. It might be a tale, an adventure or just some emotions.

2. Decide if your piece will have distinct sections or be more continuous.

3. Look at the rhythm, dynamics and special techniques you want to emphasize.

6.2 Melody and Harmony:

Craft a Melody:

1. Begin with a catchy tune. Try different segments on the Otamatone for soothing combinations.

2. Analyze the beat of your melody – it can greatly affect how your composition may feel.

3. Try ascending and descending patterns, implement a range of methods including vibrato and pitch bends.

Add Harmony:

1. Once you have your melody try adding some harmony. To create a fuller sound, use chords or layered segments.

2. Play around with a variety of chord progressions to discover what works well in tandem with your melody.

3. Think about the effect that different harmonies have on emotions – do you want your composition to be cheerful, melancholic or adventurous sounding?.

6.3 Rhythm and Dynamics:
Craft the Rhythm:

1. Create a rhythmical pattern that complements your melody and harmony.

2. Experiment with different durations of notes, pauses and patterns.

3. Use staccato and legato with strategy to improve the rhythm.

Play with Dynamics:

1. Add a dynamic variation, peaks and valleys to your composition.

2. Identify areas that can be improved or refined.

3. Try sudden dynamic changes to relay impact or smoother transitions with gradual shifts.

6.4 Form and Structure:

Define the Form:

1. Decide on the overall structure of your composition – will it be composed of an introduction, several sections or a recurring motif?

2. Determine the length that each section should take and how they flow into one another.

Create a Cohesive Structure:

1. Make sure the sections flow smoothly by incorporating thematic aspects or variations.

2. Try different types A-B-A, Rondo or your own structure.

6.5 Experiment with Advanced Techniques:

Incorporate Advanced Techniques:

1. Use advanced techniques from Chapter 5 vibrato, dynamics variation , pitch bending , staccato and legato.

2. Use these techniques to perform individual details in your composition and imbue them with expressiveness or character.

6.6 Recording and Refining:

Record Your Composition:

1. Record your performance using a recording device.

2. This will serve as a template to use in analyzing and revising your composition.

Listen and Refine:

1. Listen to your recording critically.

2. Identify areas that can be enhanced or polished.

3. Try various takes in order to find the one that fits your vision most adequately.

6.7 Conclusion:

Creating music for the Otamatone is very intimate and creative. Be open to new ways of making music, have faith in yourself and let your musical personality shine. Keep in mind that there are no strict rules; let your fantasy assist you while creating the musical piece of yours on this fanciful instrument.

In the following chapters, we will delve deeper into particular genres as well as styles to continue inspiring you for your journey of composition. Bring your little musical ideas to life on the Otamatone, and enjoy this process!

6.8 Sharing and Seeking Feedback:

Share with Others:

1. When you feel satisfied with your composition, think about sharing it friends , family or other musicians.

2. Sharing your work can get you perspectives and insights that may help refine the composition even further.

3. Be open to constructive feedback and be willing for ideas that could improve your work.

Collaborate with Other Musicians:

1. If possible work with other musicians who play different instruments.

2. Incorporating various instruments in your composition can lend a richer and more dynamic feel.

3. Collaboration efforts can also produce extraordinary music results.

6.9 Notation and Documentation:

Document Your Composition:

1. Write down a notation of your composition in writing indicating melody, harmonies and any particular techniques used.

2. Write in standard music notation or create a simplified system of symbols that you prefer.

3. Recording your composition will help you to be able later on in time not only remember what was said but also pass it officially correct with others.

6.10 Exploring Genre-specific Elements:

Consider Different Genres:

1. Consider writing in various styles – ranging from classical and jazz to pop or experimental.

2. Every genre has its specific set of conventions and possibilities for expression.

3. Playing with different genres and styles can help to grow your musical intelligence in compositional matters.

Infuse Genre-specific Elements:

1. Research the unique aspects that characterize your selected genre.

2. Use these elements in your composition and adjust them to the peculiarities of the Otamatone.

3. This can be in terms of genre-specific rhythms, harmonies and playing techniques.

6.11 Advanced Composition Techniques:

Experiment with Unconventional Sounds:

1. Experiment with very odd sounds and approaches on the Otamatone.

2. Use percussive effects, extended techniques or even electronic ones.

3. Push the limits of what an Otamatone can do, and come up with a truly special composition.

Develop Themes and Motifs:

1. Create reoccurring themes or motifs in your composition.

2. Thematic elements provide cohesiveness and unity throughout the piece.

3. Play with these themes and their changes.

6.12 Conclusion:

The Otamatone allows composing a music piece of your own as an unlimited journey in the world of creativity and self-expression. As you follow the process, embrace this quirky instrument in its individuality and let your mind wander. Be it a simple melody or an elaborate composition, every note is your opportunity to tell the story of your music.

Specific genres and advanced composition techniques will be studied more in detail throughout the following chapters. Never stop experimenting, polishing and above all else savour the path of making music with an Otamatone.

6.13 Tips on Songwriting and Arranging for the Otamatone:

Understand the Otamatone's Range:

1. Familiarize yourself with the Otamatone's pitch range, from high to low registers.

2. Investigate how varying segments impact the overall tonal color.

3. Utilize the unique sonic characteristics of the Otamatone to your advantage when crafting melodies and harmonies.

Embrace Simplicity:

1. Start with simple and catchy tunes.

2. Simplicity could be strong, especially on an instrument with a unique sound such as the Otamatone.

3. Concentrate on making strong foundation first.

Experiment with Articulation:

1. Use articulation techniques such as staccato and legato to determine the character of your composition.

2. Try using various timings and durations of notes to produce a lively performance.

3. Articulation gives nuance and personality to your music.

Explore Various Genres:

1. Do not stick to a particular genre – Otamatone is quite universal and can be used in various styles.

2. Play around with genres you like or try new ones to expand your compositional arsenal.

3. Each genre provides different opportunities for creating passionate and evocative music.

Consider Timbral Variation:

1. Change the pressure applied to the touch-sensitive strip for varying timbral qualities.

2. Apply timbral changes to express feelings or emphasise certain parts of your composition.

3. Timbral variation adds depth and interest to your arrangements.

Create Contrast:

1. Use dynamics, pitch range and rhythmic patterns for contrasting your composition.

2. The contrasting elements provide tension and release so that the listener is not bored.

3. Try sudden changes and smoothing transitions to maximize the musical movement.

Experiment with Orchestration:

1. If you are working with other musicians or instrument, think about your music's arrangement.

2. Give different instruments roles to have a balanced and textured arrangement.

3. Even if you compose for a single Otamatone, think about the "orchestration" within it.

Tell a Musical Story:

1. Write your composition in a narrative form.

2. Consider the way various parts develop toward a common storyline.

3. Connect with your listeners emotionally and musically.

Balance Complexity and Playability:

1. While you are encouraged to push the boundaries, make sure your composition is paletable on Otamatone.

2. Take into consideration the limitations of an instrument and seek a middle ground between complexity and playability.

3. Because of this, practical arrangements may be what you need to make your music more significant.

Recording and Experimenting:

1. Try to experiment by using recording tools and improve your compositions.

2. Explore different interpretations and arrangements by recording multiple takes.

3. Use technology to stack tracks, place effects and improve the sonic landscape.

6.14 Conclusion:

Creating and arranging songs using the Otamatone is a joyful and imaginative process that encourages experimentation. As you traverse this musical landscape, always trust your instincts and pay heed to the peculiarities of that instrument as you learn how it can be shaped in order best to articulate unique music drenched with emotion. In the next chapters, we'll get into particular genres, sharing insights and inspiration on what your Otamatone compositions could be like. Continue writing and develop your creativity!

Chapter 7

Troubleshooting and Maintenance

In this chapter, we'll discuss typical problems that owners of Otamatone may face and offer useful tips on how to maintain your musical instrument in tip-top shape. Troubleshooting common problems and basic maintenance can improve your overall playing experience no matter if you're a beginner or an experienced player.

7.1 Uneven Sound or Intermittent Response:

Potential Causes:

1. Dirty or Sticky Surface: Dust or dirt on the touch-sensitive strip can cause irregular responses.

2. Battery Issues: Intermittent responses may be due to low battery power.

Solution:

1. Clean the Touch-sensitive Strip: Wipe lightly the touch-sensitive strip with a clean, dry cloth.

2. Check Battery Level: Check and replace the batteries or recharge them regularly to ensure constant power.

7.2 No Sound Output:

Potential Causes:

1. Battery Depletion: Due to complete battery drain, the Otamatone may fail to produce sound.

2. Connection Issues: When there are no sound outputs, it can signify loose connections or even damaged wires.

Solution:

1. Replace or Recharge Batteries: Charge the batteries or replace them with new ones.

2. Inspect Connections: Inspect the wires and connections to ensure that they aren't loose or damaged.

7.3 Distorted or Muffled Sound:

Potential Causes:

1. Damaged Speaker or Vibrator: Distorted sound may result from physical damage to the speaker or vibrator.

2. Obstructed Sound Hole: Issues with the sound hole may lead to muffled or distorted sounds.

Solution:

1. Inspect Speaker and Vibrator: Inspect for any apparent damage and replace parts where appropriate.

2. Clear Sound Hole: Clear the sound hole of any obstructions to ensure that air flows freely.

7.4 Pitch Control Issues:

Potential Causes:

1. Touch-sensitive Strip Obstruction: Dirt or residue on the touch-sensitive strip can interfere with pitch control.

2. Calibration Issues: The calibration settings may also affect the accuracy of pitch.

Solution:

1. Clean Touch-sensitive Strip: Clean the touch-sensitive strip with a dry cloth.

2. Recalibrate the Otamatone: Recalibrate the instrument in accordance with manufacturer's instructions.

7.5 Physical Damage:

Potential Causes:

1. Drops or Impacts: Physical damages can take many forms.

2. Excessive Force: Overloading on fragile parts can result in damage.

Solution:

1. Handle with Care: Never drop or impact the Otamatone.

2. Play with Gentle Pressure: Play with a moderate and steady pressure so as to not cause damage.

7.6 Maintenance Tips:

1. Regular Cleaning: Use a clean, dry cloth to periodically wipe the surfaces of your Otamatone particularly touch-sensitive strip.

2. Battery Management: Remove batteries when they are not in use for a long time to avoid leakage.

3. Safe Storage: Store the Otamatone safely or store it in a protective case to prevent accidental damage.

4. Avoid Extreme Conditions:

7.7 Conclusion:

Troubleshooting and maintenance of your Otamatone are very crucial in ensuring that the instrument lasts you a long time By addressing these common issues promptly and practicing good maintenance, you can keep your Otamatone in perfect condition so that you will not worry about the instrument while being able to create music and take advantage of its unique features at any time. If the problems continue, seek advice from professionals or contact the manufacturer for more assistance.

Maintenance Tips for Optimal Performance

To keep your Otamatone well-maintained ensures it lasts long and continues to function properly. By using these simple initiatives, you will be able to keep your tool well maintained and benefit from its somewhat peculiar appeal as a musical instrument.

7.8 Cleaning and Care:

1. Wipe the Touch-sensitive Strip: Clean the touch-sensitive strip with a dry, lint-free cloth regularly to remove dust and residue. This ensures that they give correct responses during the game.

2. Clean the Body and Neck: Clean the body and neck of Otamatone with a clean, wet cloth. Avoid overly moisturizing, and always dry the instrument completely before playing or putting away.

 3. Care for the Sound Hole: Clear the sound hole of any debris or obstruction. use a soft brush or lightly blow air into the sound hole to clear off particles.

7.9 Battery Management:

1. Remove Batteries When Not in Use: If you are not going to play the Otamatone for a long time, take out batteries so they could not leak. This is especially crucial in cases where the instrument has been kept under different temperature.

2. Use High-Quality Batteries: Invest in high-quality batteries to ensure stable power and improved overall performance. Replenish them as soon as they are depleted.

3. Check Battery Contacts: Inspect the battery contacts periodically for signs of corrosion. If corrosion is present, clean the contacts with a little rubbing alcohol and cotton swab.

7.10 Storage Practices:

1. Protective Case: It is also worth mentioning that the Otamatone could be protected from dust, scratches and small impacts during storage by purchasing a protective case.

2. Safe Environment: Keep the Otamatone in a cool dry place out of direct sunlight, and away from extremes of temperature. Do not subject the instrument to humidity so that it does not suffer possible damage.

7.11 Calibration and Adjustment:
1. Recalibrate as Needed: Watch for pitch control problems or irregular reactions and re-calibrate the Otamatone according to manufacturer's directions. Accurate performance can be ensured by regular recalibration.
2. Check for Loose Parts: Check the Otamatone for loose screws, buttons or parts from time to time. Adjusting them to ensure proper stability.

7.12 Preventive Measures:
1. Gentle Playing Pressure: Press the Otamatone moderately and gently. Do not apply too much force on fragile parts, especially to the touch-sensitive strips.

2. Avoid Dropping: Manipulate the Otamatone gently and do not drop it on the floor. A protective case can provide additional safety in the event of accidental impacts.

3. Follow Manufacturer Guidelines: Follow the manufacturer's guidelines and recommendations for care, maintenance, usage. Following them will help you take the best possible care of your instrument.

7.13 Regular Inspection:

1. Visual Inspection: Check your Otamatone visually from time to time. Check the instrument for any signs of wear, damage or changes in appearance.

2. Listen for Abnormalities: Observe the noise made during play. Any drastic alterations or deviations could indicate deeper problems that require intervention.

7.14 Conclusion:

By following these recommendations on maintenance, you will help your Otamatone to last long and work effectively. Remember the importance of preventive measures and regular care to this unique instrument in order to preserve its charm as well as instruments function. Have a good time making sure your Otamatone continues producing the goofy noises that bring fun to all of your musical aspirations!

Conclusion:

In this book journey, we've taken a full course of exploring the Otamatone; uncovering its quirky appeal and revealing tips tricks on becoming sophisticated players and innovative composers. Let's recap the key points that have enriched our understanding of this unique instrument:

1. Introduction to the Otamatone:

- Read about the history and construction of the Otamatone, its fun characteristics.

2. Playing Basics:

- Assembled the Otamatone and touched upon basic music terminology.

3. Playing Techniques:

- Read up on different playing techniques such as finger placement, pitch control and detailed expressive touches that improved our ability to create delicate performances.

4. Understanding Otamatone Notation:

- Created a simplified notation system designed for the Otamatone, allowing players to read and understand music that has been written specifically with the instrument in mind.

5. Basic Songs and Melodies:

- A set of easy, attention-grabbing songs in addition to specific guidelines for learning and developing abilities.

6. Advanced Techniques:

- Learned advanced technique of playing instruments including the use of vibrato, dynamics variation, pitch bending ,staccato and legato which improved our capability to communicate emotions as well at smaller details during performances.

7. Creating Your Own Music:

- Guided aspiring composers through the process of crafting original compositions for the Otamatone, encouraging experimentation and self-expression.

8. Troubleshooting and Maintenance:

- Explained common issues a player may face and suggested reasonable solutions for problem solving, also provided advice on how to keep the Otamatone in top working condition.

9. Conclusion:

- The main takeaways summarized are the necessity of regular maintenance, careful playing and to follow what manufacturer tells one in a pleasurable yet long-lasting Otamatone activity. Regardless of whether you're a novice who only wants to touch upon the basics or an experienced adventurer seeking challenges in your expression, Otamatone celebrates its uniqueness and encourages you add your musical personality into its playful soundscape.

It's an instrument that lives on experimentation, creativity, and the pleasure of making music.

Here's an encouraging nudge to keep you inspired on your Otamatone adventure:

Keep Practicing:

- But practice makes perfect; keep learning new melodies, trying techniques and even setting yourself challenges. The more you play, the deeper secrets and potentials of this lovely instrument will open up to your eyes.

Embrace Creativity:

- The Otamatone is not simply a musical instrument, it's your own platform for creativity. Do it toImplement your own musical personality, compose songs and experiment with the sounds that are relevant for you in terms of feelings and fantasy.

Connect with Others:

- Record and share your Otamatone journey with other hobbyists, musicians out there. Collaboration creates new ways of inspiration and study. Connect with online communities, network collaborations and allow your music to echo outside of your personal practice sessions.

Explore Different Genres:

- The Otamatone is highly versatile i.e., it can relate to any genre and style of music. Try various kinds of music – classical, jazz and pops far beyond. Each genre brings its own difficulties and motifs.

Create Original Pieces:

- Don't be afraid of letting your creativity go where it wants to namely in original compositions. Regardless of whether you are composing a short melodic sketch or fully fledged piece, the Otamatone gives you an opportunity to make your own unique musical fingerprint.

Celebrate Your Progress:

- Even if it is small, do not forget to appreciate your progress. Every upgrade, every new technique mastered and each orchestral composition written clearly reflects how committed you are towards Otamatone.

Stay Curious:

- The Otamatone is an instrument of interest. Try out all kinds of sounds, adopt unorthodox approaches and let your imagination create new music that you have never heard before.

Remember the Joy:

- In the end, what makes playing of Otamatone so enjoyable is its sheer joyfulness. Enjoy the playful spirit of Otamatone whether you're playing for yourself or sharing your tunes.

In the vast symphony of your musical journey, Otamatone plays an eccentric and mischievous role. So come on, keep your fingers jumping up and down along the surface of this touch sensitive strip – let those tunes roll out like a tide across an ocean just for me… & hellip; and you dear folks everywhere hearing these joyous sounds only that wonderfully quirky Otamatone can make. Your musical journey has just started, and your opportunities are limitless as the sky is deep. Happy playing!

Made in the USA
Las Vegas, NV
23 December 2024

15208320R00056